About the Creators of This Calendar

Dawn Huffaker is an established poet who has written for more than 30 years. She primarily writes about the incredible beauty in nature. Her goal is to paint a memorable picture with her words. This is her seventh calendar. So far, she has published three books of poetry available at Amazon. Learn more about her at www.dawnhuffaker.com

Dawn is unable to walk. She lives her life from a motorized wheelchair. Doing photography is quite diffi-cult for her. She focuses on her poetry, instead.

Since she is unable to take her own photos, Dawn has been blessed with a family that is very talented with a camera. This year, the calendar includes beautiful nature photography from her parents, Marilyn & Ron Huffaker. They each add much to Dawn's poetry.

Photo by Marilyn Huffaker

January Wobbles

January wobbles in
With bleary eyes
From too much celebrating,
And far too little sleep.

It seeks the quiet of solitude
When the ground is covered white;
Low-hanging clouds
Catch in the weary trees;
Fog floats freely,
Skimming softly, secretly
Among sleeping mountain sentinels;
The sun sleeps in late,
Then turns in early; and
Animals dream of the coming spring warmth.

January carries the solitude
Like an invalid uses a shawl.
The world stays still and cold
While he recovers from his merrymaking.

– Dawn L. Huffaker

January 2016

December 2015
S M T W T F S
1 2 3 4 5
6 7 8 9 10 11 12
13 14 15 16 17 18 19
20 21 22 23 24 25 26
27 28 29 30 31

February 2016
S M T W T F S
1 2 3 4 5 6
7 8 9 10 11 12 13
14 15 16 17 18 19 20
21 22 23 24 25 26 27
28 29

Sunday	Monday	Tuesday	Wednesday	Thursday	Friday	Saturday
					1 New Year's Day	2
3	4	5	6	7	8	9
10	11	12	13	14	15	16
17	18 Martin Luther King, Jr., Day	19	20	21	22	23
24	25	26	27	28	29	30
31						

Bashful February

Days continue to grow longer.
The snowy grip is starting to slip.
Seeds and bulbs begin to stir.
They sense that spring is creeping nearer.

Brave hyacinths seek the timid sunshine.
Tender shoots climb above the chilled soil.
Their colorful flowers shyly look around them.
The stoic winter will soon be forgotten.

Bashful February is welcoming the coming spring.

– Dawn L. Huffaker

February 2016

January 2016

S	M	T	W	T	F	S
					1	2
3	4	5	6	7	8	9
10	11	12	13	14	15	16
17	18	19	20	21	22	23
24	25	26	27	28	29	30
31						

March 2016

S	M	T	W	T	F	S
		1	2	3	4	5
6	7	8	9	10	11	12
13	14	15	16	17	18	19
20	21	22	23	24	25	26
27	28	29	30	31		

Sunday	Monday	Tuesday	Wednesday	Thursday	Friday	Saturday
	1 National Freedom Day	2 Groundhog Day	3	4	5	6
7	8	9 Mardi Gras	10 Ash Wednesday	11	12 Lincoln's Birthday	13
14 Valentine's Day	15 Susan B. Anthony Day President's Day	16	17	18	19	20
21	22 Washington's Birthday	23	24	25	26	27
28	29 Leap Day					

Vivacious Laugh

Daylight is catching up with the dark of night.
Winter is waning in his immobilizing power.
Spring soon seeks to start her energetic reign.

Life is returning to this part of the world.
Plants peek above the warming ground.
Deciduous trees unfurl their tiny leaves.
Curious caterpillars travel to and fro-
Voraciously nibbling on tender, tasty greens.
Bees eagerly seek sustaining blossoms and blooms.
Hibernating critters begin to awaken-
Hungry are they, and eager to start hunting breakfast.

Each day is a snapshot of this magical change.
Winter's sleep and isolation are vanquished-
Replaced by Spring's vivacious laugh.

- Dawn L. Huffaker

March 2016

February 2016

S	M	T	W	T	F	S
	1	2	3	4	5	6
7	8	9	10	11	12	13
14	15	16	17	18	19	20
21	22	23	24	25	26	27
28	29					

April 2016

S	M	T	W	T	F	S
					1	2
3	4	5	6	7	8	9
10	11	12	13	14	15	16
17	18	19	20	21	22	23
24	25	26	27	28	29	30

Sunday	Monday	Tuesday	Wednesday	Thursday	Friday	Saturday
		1	2	3	4	5
6	7	8	9	10	11	12
13 Daylight Saving Begins	14	15	16	17 St. Patrick's Day	18	19
20 Palm Sunday	21 Spring Begins	22	23	24	25 Good Friday	26
27 Easter Sunday	28	29	30	31		

Peeking Out

Pear buds reach out from the waking branches.
Slowly swelling, they grow and grow.
Spring sunshine soothes and caresses them-
Making them feel safe and loved like a mother does.

Bright white petals begin peeking out among the new leaves.
Encouragement from the bees and butterflies
Brings them out of their sheltering buds.
Light and shadow dances across the blossoms in the breeze.

Sleepy pear tree is no more.
Rejuvenated and energized from winter rest,
She is eager to bring forth the blessing of her kind-
To create her seeds for progeny and fruit for fauna fare.

– Dawn L. Huffaker

Photo by Marilyn Huffaker.

April 2016

March 2016
S M T W T F S
        1 2 3 4 5
6 7 8 9 10 11 12
13 14 15 16 17 18 19
20 21 22 23 24 25 26
27 28 29 30 31

May 2016
S M T W T F S
1 2 3 4 5 6 7
8 9 10 11 12 13 14
15 16 17 18 19 20 21
22 23 24 25 26 27 28
29 30 31

Sunday	Monday	Tuesday	Wednesday	Thursday	Friday	Saturday
					1 April Fool's Day	2
3	4	5	6	7	8	9
10	11	12	13	14	15	16
17	18	19	20	21	22 Earth Day	23
24	25	26	27 Administrative Assistant's Day	28	29 Arbor Day	30

Pale Pink Petals

Pale pink petals open to the morning sun.
A new day has begun in the garden for Rose.
Butterflies softly land to admire her beauty.
Ladybugs wave to her as they pass by.

Little junco bird lands near Rose.
He chirps a happy song for all to hear.
Rose beams at his warbling serenade.
Serenity and contentment make her complete.

— Dawn L. Huffaker

May 2016

Sunday	Monday	Tuesday	Wednesday	Thursday	Friday	Saturday
1	2	3 **National Teacher Day**	4	5 **Cinco de Mayo**	6	7
8 **Mother's Day**	9	10	11	12	13	14
15	16	17	18	19	20	21 **Armed Forces Day**
22 **National Maritime Day**	23	24	25	26	27	28
29	30 **Memorial Day**	31				

Dainty Parasols

Soft spring sun slowly shifts to summer simmer.
Plants stretch and preen before her.
Soon the sunlight is too inviting for sunbathing.

Tiny buds grow above the leaves.
Petals open up to the hot summer sky-
Resembling the dainty parasols of yore.

Young plants quickly become mature.
Hummingbirds and bees collect pollen or nectar from each.
Parasol flowers glisten glamorously sharing their beauty.

— *Dawn L. Huffaker*

Photo by Marilyn Huffaker

June 2016

May 2016

S	M	T	W	T	F	S
1	2	3	4	5	6	7
8	9	10	11	12	13	14
15	16	17	18	19	20	21
22	23	24	25	26	27	28
29	30	31				

July 2016

S	M	T	W	T	F	S
					1	2
3	4	5	6	7	8	9
10	11	12	13	14	15	16
17	18	19	20	21	22	23
24	25	26	27	28	29	30
31						

Sunday	Monday	Tuesday	Wednesday	Thursday	Friday	Saturday
			1	2	3	4
5	6	7	8	9	10	11
12	13	14 Flag Day	15	16	17	18
19 Father's Day	20	21 Summer Begins	22	23	24	25
26	27	28	29	30		

Fourth of July Fireworks

Slide! Bud sneaks out from below the cactus stickers.
Pop! Iridescent pink cactus flower blooms gracefully.
Sigh! Such color brings incredible beauty to this special day.

Whoosh! Flash of light shoots up to the dark night sky.
Bang! The firework blossoms brilliantly.
Ooh! Sparkles of color slowly fade to smoke and ash.

Each celebrates their freedom in their own special way.
Each makes our country better because they are here.
Each is free to become who they were meant to be.

Happy Fourth of July!

     - Dawn L. Huffaker

Photo by Marilyn Huffaker

July 2016

June 2016

S	M	T	W	T	F	S
			1	2	3	4
5	6	7	8	9	10	11
12	13	14	15	16	17	18
19	20	21	22	23	24	25
26	27	28	29	30		

August 2016

S	M	T	W	T	F	S
	1	2	3	4	5	6
7	8	9	10	11	12	13
14	15	16	17	18	19	20
21	22	23	24	25	26	27
28	29	30	31			

Sunday	Monday	Tuesday	Wednesday	Thursday	Friday	Saturday
					1	2
3	4 **Independence Day**	5	6	7	8	9
10	11	12	13	14	15	16
17	18	19	20	21	22	23
24 **Parent's Day**	25	26	27	28	29	30
31						

Paint the Promise

Shades of gray paint the promise
Of a coming summer storm.
Clouds come together quickly
To discuss their battle plan.
How much rain to deliver?
Will there be hail? How big?
Where do the lightning strikes go?

When the sun exits the sky,
The clouds begin their performance.
Pitter patter, the raindrops slowly fall,
Making sweet music like a heavenly orchestra does.
Lightning flashes brilliantly to make the clear drops
Twinkle like tantalizing diamonds on every surface.
Thunder grumbles deeply like a grouchy kettle drum.

Raindrops begin to fall faster and faster.
Lightning turns into a strobe light.
Descending drops dance like ballerinas on pointed toes.
Thunder picks up the beat heading toward a crescendo.
Animals dash for cover. Wait for the sun to return.
Fallen drops begin to pool together in puddles.
Dust disappears off of refreshed leaves and branches.

Thunder murmurs in the distance.
Dancing drops move slower now.
Fewer dancers join the dance.
Clouds begin to part and move on
Allowing the sun to take his throne again.
Peering down on the spectacular scene below,
The sun king blissfully smiles at such beauty.

— *Dawn L. Huffaker*

August 2016

July 2016
S M T W T F S
          1 2
3 4 5 6 7 8 9
10 11 12 13 14 15 16
17 18 19 20 21 22 23
24 25 26 27 28 29 30
31

September 2016
S M T W T F S
        1 2 3
4 5 6 7 8 9 10
11 12 13 14 15 16 17
18 19 20 21 22 23 24
25 26 27 28 29 30

Sunday	Monday	Tuesday	Wednesday	Thursday	Friday	Saturday
	1	2	3	4	5	6
7	8	9	10	11	12	13
14	15	16	17	18	19	20
21	22	23	24	25	26	27
28	29	30	31			

Deer Trail

Deer trail comes down a gentle hill.
It passes through twin tree trunks.
Young doe pauses to look around.

She dare not tarry long.
Fall is closing in upon her.
Soon the green grass and leaves
Will be but a tasty memory.

Head to earth and lips to leaves.
Nibble. Nibble. Nibble.
Gaining weight for the lean months to come.

Beautiful visitor, you grace us with your presence.
Such a delight it is when you pass by.
Thank you for being in my world!

— Dawn L. Huffaker

September 2016

August 2016

S	M	T	W	T	F	S
	1	2	3	4	5	6
7	8	9	10	11	12	13
14	15	16	17	18	19	20
21	22	23	24	25	26	27
28	29	30	31			

October 2016

S	M	T	W	T	F	S
						1
2	3	4	5	6	7	8
9	10	11	12	13	14	15
16	17	18	19	20	21	22
23	24	25	26	27	28	29
30	31					

Sunday	Monday	Tuesday	Wednesday	Thursday	Friday	Saturday
				1	2	3
4	5 Labor Day	6	7	8	9	10
11 Grandparent's Day	12	13	14	15	16 Citizenship Day	17
18	19	20	21	22 Autumn Begins	23	24
25	26	27	28	29	30	

Autumn Has Arrived

The days continue to become shorter.
Nighttime temperatures are a bit chilly.
Growing things know that they must slumber.

Virginia Creeper has braved the chill of spring.
She has gracefully spread far and wide this past summer.
Her seed progeny will make beautiful vines next year.

The time has come for her to rest.
With a sigh, she withdraws her sap from the leaves.
Leaves start changing from dark green to brilliant red.

The chill wind flutters the colorful leaves as it passes by.
As each gust goes by, more leaves float to quiet earth.
Virginia Creeper drifts off into her peaceful winter sleep.

Autumn has arrived to celebrate the harvest.
Autumn has arrived to bring rest to weary plants.
Autumn has arrived to prepare the way for winter.

– Dawn L. Huffaker

Photo by Ron Huffaker

October 2016

September 2016
S	M	T	W	T	F	S
				1	2	3
4	5	6	7	8	9	10
11	12	13	14	15	16	17
18	19	20	21	22	23	24
25	26	27	28	29	30	

November 2016
S	M	T	W	T	F	S
		1	2	3	4	5
6	7	8	9	10	11	12
13	14	15	16	17	18	19
20	21	22	23	24	25	26
27	28	29	30			

Sunday	Monday	Tuesday	Wednesday	Thursday	Friday	Saturday
						1
2	3	4	5	6	7	8
9	10 **Columbus Day**	11	12	13	14	15
16	17	18	19	20	21	22
23	24 **United Nations Day**	25	26	27	28	29
30	31 **Halloween**					

Hurry My Children

Bright Mums beam to the garden around.
They have finally made their appearance!
It had been hard work growing all summer,
Making ready for their coming-out party.

Mother Nature is proud of her children.
Each has its own unique character and personality.
Roses are delicate and shy.
Chrysanthemums are brave and bold.

The summer has come and gone.
Most of her children are now fast asleep.
The Mums have waited so long to blossom that
They are resisting her call to hurry.

A cold gust of wind ruffles their petals.
Chill bumps tickle their stems.
"Hurry my children!" says Mother Nature,
"Make ready for bed. Hurry!"

With a sigh, they fold their petals away,
And return their sap to the roots.
When the cold wind comes by yet again,
The Mums are nestled down deep - asleep for winter.

- Dawn L. Huffaker

Photo by Ron Huffaker

November 2016

October 2016
S M T W T F S
1
2 3 4 5 6 7 8
9 10 11 12 13 14 15
16 17 18 19 20 21 22
23 24 25 26 27 28 29
30 31

December 2016
S M T W T F S
1 2 3
4 5 6 7 8 9 10
11 12 13 14 15 16 17
18 19 20 21 22 23 24
25 26 27 28 29 30 31

Sunday	Monday	Tuesday	Wednesday	Thursday	Friday	Saturday
		1	2	3	4	5
6 Daylight Saving Ends	7	8 Election Day	9	10	11 Veterans Day	12
13	14	15	16	17	18	19
20	21	22	23	24 Thanksgiving Day	25	26
27	28	29	30			

Photo by Marilyn Huffaker

All Is Calm

Hustle and bustle of Christmas time
Has come to a halt.
The snow came in the dark of night.
Snowflakes have gathered in every
Nook and cranny of the sleeping trees.

All is calm.
All is quiet.
All is still.
All are in awe of the scene before them.
All feel blessed to be witnesses.

Memories of another time come forward.
A manger surrounded by three wise men
Bringing gifts for the newborn King-
Gold, frankincense, and myrrh.
Angels sang His welcome.

All was calm.
All was quiet.
All was still.
All were in awe of the scene before them.
All felt blessed to be witnesses.

Merry Christmas!

- Dawn L. Huffaker

December 2016

Sunday	Monday	Tuesday	Wednesday	Thursday	Friday	Saturday
				1	2	3
4	5	6	7	8	9	10
11	12	13	14	15 **Bill of Rights Day**	16	17
18	19	20	21 **Winter Begins**	22	23	24 **Christmas Eve**
25 **Christmas Day**	26	27	28	29	30	31 **New Year's Eve**

Notes

2017

January 2017

S	M	T	W	T	F	S
1	2	3	4	5	6	7
8	9	10	11	12	13	14
15	16	17	18	19	20	21
22	23	24	25	26	27	28
29	30	31				

February 2017

S	M	T	W	T	F	S
			1	2	3	4
5	6	7	8	9	10	11
12	13	14	15	16	17	18
19	20	21	22	23	24	25
26	27	28				

March 2017

S	M	T	W	T	F	S
			1	2	3	4
5	6	7	8	9	10	11
12	13	14	15	16	17	18
19	20	21	22	23	24	25
26	27	28	29	30	31	

April 2017

S	M	T	W	T	F	S
						1
2	3	4	5	6	7	8
9	10	11	12	13	14	15
16	17	18	19	20	21	22
23	24	25	26	27	28	29
30						

May 2017

S	M	T	W	T	F	S
	1	2	3	4	5	6
7	8	9	10	11	12	13
14	15	16	17	18	19	20
21	22	23	24	25	26	27
28	29	30	31			

June 2017

S	M	T	W	T	F	S
				1	2	3
4	5	6	7	8	9	10
11	12	13	14	15	16	17
18	19	20	21	22	23	24
25	26	27	28	29	30	

July 2017

S	M	T	W	T	F	S
						1
2	3	4	5	6	7	8
9	10	11	12	13	14	15
16	17	18	19	20	21	22
23	24	25	26	27	28	29
30	31					

August 2017

S	M	T	W	T	F	S
		1	2	3	4	5
6	7	8	9	10	11	12
13	14	15	16	17	18	19
20	21	22	23	24	25	26
27	28	29	30	31		

September 2017

S	M	T	W	T	F	S
					1	2
3	4	5	6	7	8	9
10	11	12	13	14	15	16
17	18	19	20	21	22	23
24	25	26	27	28	29	30

October 2017

S	M	T	W	T	F	S
1	2	3	4	5	6	7
8	9	10	11	12	13	14
15	16	17	18	19	20	21
22	23	24	25	26	27	28
29	30	31				

November 2017

S	M	T	W	T	F	S
			1	2	3	4
5	6	7	8	9	10	11
12	13	14	15	16	17	18
19	20	21	22	23	24	25
26	27	28	29	30		

December 2017

S	M	T	W	T	F	S
					1	2
3	4	5	6	7	8	9
10	11	12	13	14	15	16
17	18	19	20	21	22	23
24	25	26	27	28	29	30
31